THE BLACK RHINOCEROS

The black rhino's creation
Brings viewers much elation
And hope for its salvation
Throughout its home location.

This simple short narration
About our admiration
And heartfelt adoration
And strong appreciation

Should bring a celebration
To all whose aspiration
Is for its commendation
And for its preservation.

Know rhino conservation
And not its exploitation
Is our firm expectation
In this new dispensation.

1

The black rhinoceros is large,
And weighs more than a ton,

And if, to you, it starts to charge,
Then you had better run.

At speeds of up to thirty-five
In miles per hour they go.

They're agile, big, and full of drive,
So don't think they are slow.

Although its eyesight's very poor,
It hears things very well.

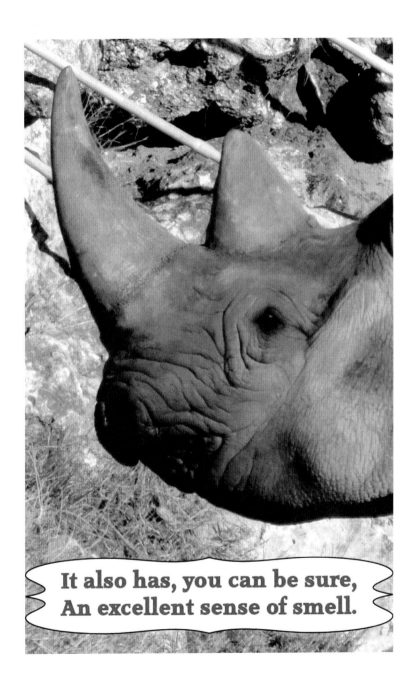

It also has, you can be sure,
An excellent sense of smell.

The black rhinoceros is not black,
But gray, or brownish gray.

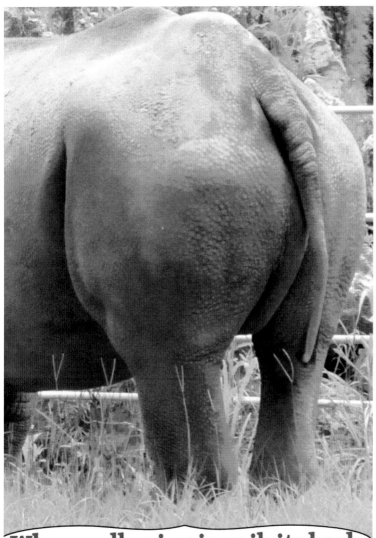

When wallowing in soil, its back
And skin turn dark, they say.

Its name may come from local soil
That covers rhino's skin

This soil is black and sticks like oil.
It shows where rhino's been.

It has two horns atop its head,
A large one and a small.

The value of these horns is said
To be rhino's downfall.

BLACK RHINOCEROS
'Diceros bicornis'

The black rhinoceros is actually gray to brownish gray, and probably derives its name from the dark colored local soil covering its skin from wallowing.

It is also known as the prehensile-lipped rhinoceros because of its flexible upper lip which allows it to pluck the leaves from trees and shrubs that make up the majority of the diet.

The rhino's two horns are its primary defense weapons and are made up of compressed fibers of keratin, which is the same substance that fingernails are made of. These horns are not attached to the skull and will regenerate if broken.

Rhinos have an excellent sense of smell and good hearing, but their eyesight is rather poor. They are surprisingly agile for such a massive animal and can run at speeds up to 35 miles per hour.

Black rhinos are relatively solitary animals as opposed to the more social white rhinoceros, which also live in Africa.

East and Southeast Africa, Northern Sudan, Northeast Nigeria

THE PARKS AT
CHEHAW

FOCUS ON THE KIDS, CREATURES
COMMUNITIES SOUTHWEST GEORGIA

Illegal poaching of its horn
Is a big rhino threat.

FACT

The largest land mammal that ever existed was an ancient species of rhinoceros, which is now extinct.

ATTACK

"Just stop," police routinely warn,
But is has not stopped, yet.

Just like our fingernails, each horn
Is made of keratin.

From compressed fibers which adorn
Its head, where it's built in.

Both horns are used for its defense,
And it will quickly fight

With any thing that gives offense,
And fight with all its might.

When broken, horns regenerate,
And grow again so they

Can let the rhino dominate,
And send their foes away.

Rhinos may live up to five days
With no water for thirst.

So when drought shows in nasty ways,
Survival skills come first.

They often wallow deep in mud
To keep their bodies cool.

They may lie down with quite a "thud,"
In their dark muddy pool.

In Africa, southeast and east,
They roam from day to day.

Northern Sudan, also, this beast
Has found a place to stay.

No natural predators are found
For this amazing brute.

Its size and deadly horns resound
With force in a dispute.

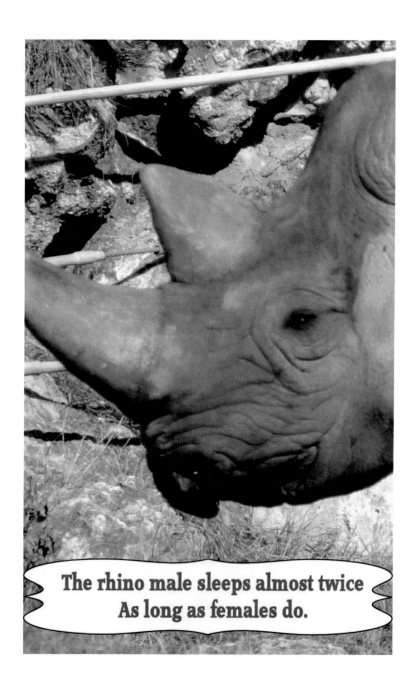

The rhino male sleeps almost twice
As long as females do.

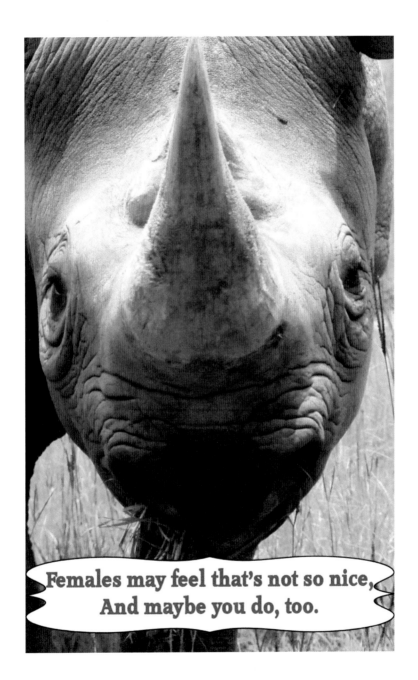

Females may feel that's not so nice,
And maybe you do, too.

The black rhino may live alone,
A solitary beast,

And for its diet, it is prone
To make a leafy feast.

Two hundred twenty types of plants
This animal will eat.

Leaves from trees and shrubs and plants
Give this big beast a treat.

Though big and strong and sometimes mean,
The black rhino is still

A wondrous animal to be seen,
It gives us all a thrill.

This book is dedicated to the staff at Chehaw Wild Animal Park and all those who who love wildlife and help to preserve it. All pictures were taken at Chehaw Wild Animal Park in Albany, Georgia.

The author, Ritchey Marbury, is a registered professional civil engineer and registered land surveyor. He loves nature and the outdoors, and hopes to instill that same love in children and adults everywhere.

Made in the USA
Las Vegas, NV
11 March 2024